It's My State!

MASSACHUSETTS

The Bay State

Ruth Bjorklund and Stephanie Fitzgerald

Cavendish
Square

New York

Published in 2015 by Cavendish Square Publishing, LLC
243 5th Avenue, Suite 136, New York, NY 10016
Copyright © 2015 by Cavendish Square Publishing, LLC

Third Edition

Library of Congress Cataloging-in-Publication Data
Bjorklund, Ruth.
Massachusetts / by Ruth Bjorklund and Stephanie Fitzgerald. — [Third Edition].
p. cm. — (It's my state!)
Includes index.
ISBN 978-1-62712-500-0 (hardcover) ISBN 978-1-62712-503-1 (ebook)
1. Massachusetts — Juvenile literature. I. Bjorklund, Ruth. II. Title.
F64.3 .B57 2015
974.4—d23

Editorial Director: Dean Miller
Editor, Third Edition: Nicole Sothard
Art Director: Jeffrey Talbot
Series Designer, Third Edition: Jeffrey Talbot
Layout Design, Third Edition: Erica Clendening
Production Manager: Jennifer Ryder-Talbot
Production Editor: David McNamara

Printed in the United States of America

MASSACHUSETTS

CONTENTS

State Flower: Mayflower

The mayflower has sweet-smelling pink or white petals and grows in the sandy and rocky soil of the state's woodlands. The mayflower has had protected status in the state since 1925.

State Dog: Boston Terrier

A cross between an English bulldog and an English terrier, the Boston terrier was the first purebred dog developed in the United States.

State Tree: American Elm

The American elm was adopted as the state tree to honor General George Washington, who took command of the Continental Army beneath an elm in Cambridge Common in 1775. This large tree with gray, flaky bark has dark green oval leaves that turn yellow in fall.

MASSACHUSETTS
POPULATION: 6,547,629

State Marine Mammal: Right Whale

Whalers considered this mammal the "right," or best, whale to hunt for its blubber, which was used to produce lamp oil. Early New Englanders hunted this whale, which swims closer to shore than most other whales, almost into extinction. Today, many people work together to protect this highly **endangered** species.

State Bird: Black-Capped Chickadee

The black-capped chickadee is one of the most familiar North American birds. This tiny flyer is only about 5 inches (13 centimeters) long, including its tail, which accounts for half its length. The gray, brown, black, and white bird often nests in stumps, in trees, or on fence posts. It is easily identified by its song—"chick-adee-dee-dee."

State Cookie: Chocolate Chip Cookie

In the 1930s, Ruth Wakefield, the owner of the Toll House Inn in Whitman, Massachusetts, tried mixing pieces of semisweet chocolate into her dough for butter cookies. Her "toll house" chocolate chip cookies became famous throughout the state as well as the nation.

A view of the water from Nantucket Island.

The Bay State

People say the name Massachusetts comes from the language of the Massachusett tribe. The words "massa" (great) and "wachusetts" (mountain) together mean "great mountain place."

Massachusetts is part of New England, a region in the northeastern part of the country that also includes Connecticut, Rhode Island, Vermont, New Hampshire, and Maine. Massachusetts contains 14 counties. Boston, the state's capital and largest city, is part of Suffolk County in the eastern part of the state.

At just 7,840 square miles (20,306 square kilometers), Massachusetts is a small state, but it has a wide variety of landforms. In fact, it has more than any other New England state. Massachusetts has many types of beaches—some are sandy and flat; others are rocky and steep. Rivers flow throughout the state, including New England's largest, the Connecticut River. There are mountain ranges, rolling farmlands, sand dunes, swamps, lakes, and forests.

Mount Greylock State Reservation, created in 1898, is Massachusetts's first wilderness state park.

Massachusetts Borders

North:	Vermont
	New Hampshire
South:	Connecticut
	Rhode Island
East:	Atlantic Ocean
West:	New York

Western Massachusetts

The scenic Berkshire Hills in western Massachusetts is a great place to enjoy the brilliant colors of fall. Hardwood trees such as oak, beech, maple, and white birch cover the hills. When the weather cools, the leaves turn many shades of yellow, red, and gold.

When it was first formed, the Berkshire mountain range featured sharp and jagged peaks. After millions of years, however, wind, ice, and water wore away the peaks. Eventually, they were worn down to only the hardest rock, creating the rounded hills that exist today. Because the ground is rugged and the soil is poor, few people have farmed this region, where beavers, bobcats, wild turkeys, snowshoe hares, porcupines, black bears, and mink live. Nearby are two large river valleys, the Hoosic and the Housatonic. These valleys feature wonderful white-water rapids, waterfalls, and sheer walls of marble, quartz, and granite. Mount Greylock, the state's highest peak, rises here. The mountain reaches 3,491 feet (1,064 meters) at its **summit**.

The Connecticut River Valley

The Connecticut River runs north to south for 68 miles (109 km) through the center of Massachusetts. The river flows by fertile farms, wetlands, dinosaur-footprint fossils, and a 300-million-year-old lava flow. Not far from the Connecticut River is a valuable natural resource called Quabbin Reservoir. In the 1930s, Boston and other big cities wanted to dam a river because they needed more fresh water. Officials asked the citizens of four nearby towns to relocate. They agreed, and their houses and businesses were moved by truck. Workers built a dam, which helped flood the abandoned towns. Today, migrating birds along with deer, coyotes, and eagles flock to Quabbin Reservoir. This wildlife refuge is full of color in spring, when thousands of dragonflies and butterflies gather.

Quabbin Reservoir covers 39 square miles (101 sq km), is 18 miles (29 km) long, and has 181 miles (291 km) of shoreline.

MASSACHUSETTS
COUNTY MAP

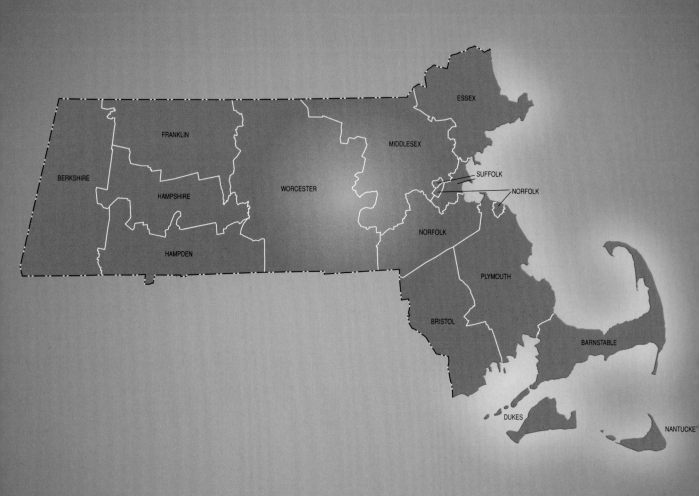

ESSEX

FRANKLIN

MIDDLESEX

BERKSHIRE

SUFFOLK

HAMPSHIRE

WORCESTER

NORFOLK

NORFOLK

HAMPDEN

PLYMOUTH

BRISTOL

BARNSTABLE

DUKES

NANTUCKE

MASSACHUSETTS
POPULATION BY COUNTY

Barnstable County	215,888
Berkshire County	131,219
Bristol County	548,285
Dukes County	16,535
Essex County	743,159
Franklin County	71,372
Hampden County	463,490
Hampshire County	158,080
Middlesex County	1,503,085
Nantucket County	10,172
Norfolk County	670,850
Plymouth County	494,919
Suffolk County	722,023
Worcester County	798,552

Source: U.S. Bureau of the Census, 2010

Berkshire County

Suffolk County

Boston, in Eastern Massachusetts, is the largest city in the state.

Eastern Massachusetts

Although Eastern Massachusetts is the most populated area of the state, it has lots of natural places to explore. Along the North Shore, birders come from all over the world to watch for the thousands of shorebirds that live in the marshes, sand dunes, and wetlands. The fishing communities of Gloucester and Rockport are located on Cape Ann, which juts into the sea. From Cape Ann to north of Boston, the coastline is rocky, with many small islands. Boston and its far-reaching suburbs are built along the shores of Boston Harbor. Two major rivers, the Mystic and the Charles, flow into the harbor. During the last Ice Age, which ended about 11,500 years ago, glaciers covered the coastline from what is now Boston to Cape Cod, carving out ponds, rock ledges, and river valleys. When Earth's climate warmed, the glaciers drew back, leaving behind small rocks and giant boulders. The most famous of these boulders is Plymouth Rock.

Cape Cod

American writer Henry David Thoreau called Cape Cod "the bare and bended arm of Massachusetts." Cape Cod, located at the easternmost part of Massachusetts, stretches 65 miles (105 km) into the Atlantic Ocean. All along the Cape, there are forests, swamps, salt marshes, sandy beaches, cliffs, and dunes. The outward side of the "arm" faces east to the Atlantic. Tides and storms pound the shoreline, pushing the sand into fantastic shapes. A series of islands, including Nantucket, Martha's Vineyard, and the Elizabeth Islands, lie to the south in Nantucket Sound. On the inside of the "arm's" curve, salt marshes and cranberry bogs line the shores of Cape Cod Bay.

Provincetown, on the tip of Cape Cod, is a popular tourist destination.

10 KEY SITES ★ ★ ★

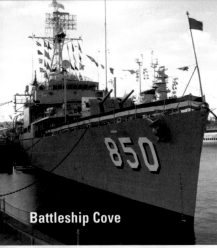

Battleship Cove

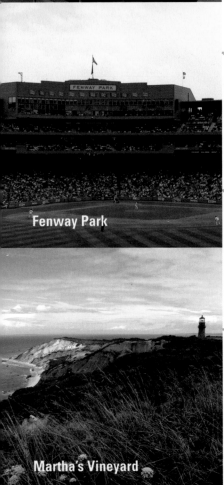

Fenway Park

Martha's Vineyard

1. Battleship Cove

Located in Fall River, Battleship Cove is a military ship museum and war memorial. It features the largest collection of preserved U.S. Navy ships in the world, which includes a battleship, destroyer, and a submarine.

2. Blue Hills Reservation

Blue Hills Reservation is a 7,000-acre (2,833-hectares) park that is just miles from downtown Boston. There are more than 125 miles (201 km) of trails there, and at the park's summit, visitors can look over most of the city.

3. Fenway Park

The historic home of the Boston Red Sox, Fenway Park is the oldest ballpark in Major League Baseball. Opened in 1912, Fenway Park is best known for its hand-operated scoreboard and the "Green Monster," a 37-foot (11-m) wall in left field.

4. Freedom Trail

The Freedom Trail is a 2.5-mile (4-km) path that leads visitors to 16 historical locations in Boston. Some of the sites include Boston Common, the site of the Boston Massacre, the Old North Church, and Paul Revere's house.

5. Martha's Vineyard

Nicknamed "The Vineyard," Martha's Vineyard is a 100-square mile (259-sq km) island that is a popular place for locals and tourists to spend the summer. It is only accessible by air or boat. During the summer, the population grows from around 15,000 to around 100,000.

6. New England Aquarium

With more than 1.3 million visitors a year, the New England Aquarium is one of the most visited attractions in Boston. Among its many exhibits is the Giant Tank, a 200,000-gallon (257,000-liters) Caribbean habitat that houses more than 1,000 animals.

7. Old Sturbridge Village

Old Sturbridge Village, in Sturbridge, is a living history museum that recreates what life was like in an 1830s rural New England town. The village features more than 40 original buildings, including a school, bank, store, homes, and working farm.

8. Salem Witch Museum

At the Salem Witch Museum, visitors learn about the witch trials that happened in Salem in 1692. The museum features life-sized figures that help depict the story. There are also guides who talk about what the term "witch" has meant throughout history.

9. Tanglewood

Located in the town of Lenox, in the Berkshires, Tanglewood is a music venue and the summer home of the Boston Symphony Orchestra. From June through Labor Day, visitors enjoy classical, folk, rock, and jazz concerts.

10. Walden Pond

From 1845 to 1847, writer Henry David Thoreau lived on the north shore of Walden Pond, near Concord. His experience provided the material for his book, *Walden*. Today, visitors hike, take tours, swim, and enjoy the natural beauty of the lake and surrounding woods.

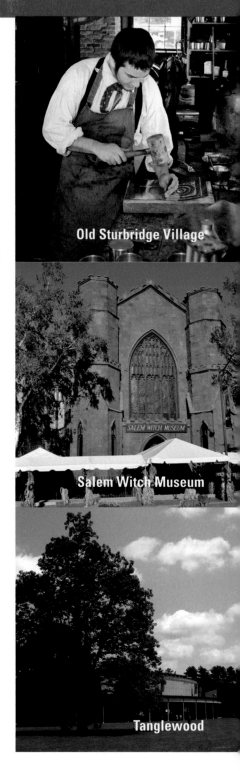

Old Sturbridge Village

Salem Witch Museum

Tanglewood

A man tries to shovel out his car after a snowstorm hits Boston.

The Four Seasons

It is not only the landscape in Massachusetts that offers a lot of variety. Residents of this New England state enjoy a full range of seasons—winter, spring, summer, and fall. "I truly think the most beautiful part of the country is here. We have great winters, wonderful summers, mountains, the shore, and Cape Cod. It is unique," says a proud resident.

In summer, Massachusetts has consistent temperatures. Many summer days are humid and sticky. In fall, days are cool and crisp, with clear blue skies. Leaves turn dazzling colors. When winter sets in, nights grow long, and the average temperature drops to 30 degrees Fahrenheit (-1 degree Celsius). Lakes and ponds freeze over, and snowfall can be as much as 67 inches (170 cm) a year in the colder mountainous areas. Spring is the shortest season. There may be frost on the ground as late as May.

Year-round, the ocean affects the climate along the coast. On a hot summer day, beachgoers enjoy cool breezes from the sea. In winter, coastal temperatures are usually warmer than inland. But nor'easters can roar across the North Atlantic Ocean and hit the beach with terrific force. Nor'easters blast coastal towns with heavy snowfalls and fallen trees, causing floods and power outages.

Wildlife and Water

Massachusetts features thousands of miles (km) of seashore and riverbanks, as well as many wetlands, lakes, and ponds. Average rainfall in the state is 44 inches (112 cm), which is enough to keep most swamps, marshes, and rivers from going dry. These areas have long been home to a variety of Massachusetts's wildlife.

Since the 1860s, factories and towns have crowded the shores and riverbanks of the state's waterways. Waste from homes and factories has polluted rivers, lakes, streams, harbors, bays, and the ocean itself. Over time, many native species have died off completely, while others have become threatened or endangered. In 1988, President George H. W. Bush called Boston Harbor "the filthiest harbor in America." But Massachusetts residents took charge. After a multibillion-dollar cleanup effort, Boston Harbor is no longer an oozing, smelly mess. The water is cleaner. Native fish species are back, and sea life is healthier. Swimmers, boaters, and beachcombers have returned.

President John F. Kennedy created the Cape Cod National Seashore in 1961. It has more than 43,000 acres (17,400 ha) of beaches, ponds, and woods.

A piping plover searches for food on a beach.

Today's citizens are also working to repair damage to the wild areas of Cape Cod. Early settlers, the Pilgrims, created Cape Cod's famous dunes when they cut down the trees for pastureland. Crashing waves and strong winds turned the treeless land into a sandy, desertlike place. At first, the sand was in danger of washing away. But beach grasses grew, holding the sand in place and protecting the habitats of the Cape's creatures—red foxes, coyotes, great horned owls, marsh hawks, blue herons, hognose snakes, herring gulls, and piping plovers. Still, some beach dwellers continue to be at risk.

The U.S. government lists the piping plover, a tiny bird, as threatened in Massachusetts. (People must take special steps to protect threatened or endangered plants and animals.) Cape Cod residents have closed off sections of beach where the plovers make their nests. Thanks to these efforts, the piping plover population is growing.

Another endangered species is the northern red-bellied cooter, formerly known as the Plymouth redbelly turtle. This reptile has trouble sharing its home with human neighbors. Redbellies live mainly in ponds but nest in forests and meadows. As human populations have increased, the turtles have lost protected nesting sites. The turtles' eggs—and tiny hatchlings—are especially vulnerable to predators such as skunks and raccoons. Predators destroy as many as half the cooters' nests each year.

In 1980, the Natural Heritage and Endangered Species Program (part of the Massachusetts Division of Fisheries and Wildlife) began a special effort to save the northern red-bellied cooter. Each fall, biologists collect about 100 hatchlings from their nests. They raise the tiny baby turtles in captivity for the first year and then release the turtles into the wild. Thanks to this special treatment, the yearlings are the size of three-year-old turtles when they are set free. Large cooters are less likely to be preyed upon and have a better chance of surviving to adulthood.

A Fish and Wildlife Service worker and a volunteer examine baby cooters, which are just 1 inch (2.5 cm) long when they hatch.

Beaver

Huckleberry

Humpback Whale

1. State Tree: American Elm

Also known as the white elm or soft elm, the American elm can reach to 98 to 125 feet (30 to 38 m) in height. The tree's wood is hard, which makes it difficult to chop. Because of this, the American elm is not often used to build things.

2. Beaver

For thousands of years, beavers gnawed young trees to build lodges and dams throughout Massachusetts. However, years of trapping caused beavers to disappear from the state from the late 1700s to the early 1900s. After an effort to restore beavers to the region, populations were up again by the 1950s.

3. State Bird: Black-Capped Chickadee

These chickadees are curious birds. They are known for, after some training, taking seeds out of humans' hands. Chickadees are found in any habitats that have trees and shrubs, from forests to parks and backyards.

4. Huckleberry

A tasty ingredient in pies and muffins, the huckleberry is also a treat for bears and the caterpillars that turn into butterflies. Henry David Thoreau once wrote, "This crop grows wild all over the country, wholesome, bountiful, and free, a real ambrosia."

5. Humpback Whale

The acrobatic and endangered humpback whale is a favorite among Massachusetts's whale-watchers. Humpbacks can grow to 60 feet (18 m) long, weigh up to 40 tons (36,000 kilograms), and eat about 5,000 pounds (2,300 kg) of plankton, krill, and fish a day!

MASSACHUSETTS

6. State Flower: Mayflower

The mayflower became the state flower in 1918. It grows along the ground, and it prefers shady areas. The mayflower's leaves were once used to make wreaths.

7. Snowy Tree Cricket

On summer evenings, the male snowy tree cricket chirps loudly to attract a mate. Also called the "thermometer cricket," a person can estimate the temperature by counting its chirps. Count the number of chirps heard in a 13-second interval and add 40 to get the current temperature in degrees Fahrenheit.

8. Spotted Salamander

In the spring, spotted salamanders come out of the ground and travel to pools of water, where they breed. Unfortunately, roadways pose a major threat. State **environmentalists** have created special tunnels to help the salamanders cross under roadways.

9. State Insect: Two-Spotted Ladybug

Two-spotted ladybugs are round, red beetles with two black spots on their bodies. They are 0.16 to 0.24 inches (4 to 6 millimeters) long, and they can be found in gardens and in the woods.

10. White Oak

For many, the white oak tree represents strength, power, stateliness, and grace. In colonial times, people often gathered to meet, teach, or sign important documents under the protective branches of a tall oak. The decks of Massachusetts's most powerful warship, the USS *Constitution* (also known as Old Ironsides), were made of white oak.

Snowy Tree Cricket

Spotted Salamander

White Oak

Native Americans welcome the Puritans on the Charles River in the 1630s.

From the Beginning

Many millions of years ago, what we now call Massachusetts was a warm rain forest, full of dinosaurs and other prehistoric creatures. In other periods of the state's geologic history, the climate was much colder. In these ice-age periods, the land was buried beneath a thick layer of ice. When the last Ice Age ended about 11,500 years ago, plants and animals again thrived in the area, and exciting things began to happen.

The First People

The first people who lived in present-day Massachusetts arrived there about 11,000 years ago. They made stone weapons for hunting and gathered nuts and berries from the forests and shellfish from the beaches. About 2,000 to 3,000 years ago, several Algonquian-speaking tribes settled along the streams and rivers of what is now Massachusetts. They began to form semipermanent villages. The people lived in lodges and wigwams, which they made by stretching tree bark and animal hides over wooden frames. They grew crops, hunted, and fished, moving with the seasons to take advantage of different food sources. Algonquian tribes living near the sea caught fish and hunted whales. Those living on Cape Cod were called the Nausets. Other Algonquians were the Patuxet, Wampanoag, and Nipmuc tribes.

The Pilgrims board the *Mayflower* before their journey.

Europeans Arrive

Historians believe that about a thousand years ago, Norse explorers might have been the first Europeans to view the lands that would become Massachusetts. About 500 years went by before other European explorers reached what is now New England. The Italian explorer Giovanni da Verrazzano **surveyed** the northeast coast of North America in 1524. In the next century, John Smith (who had founded the Jamestown colony in Virginia in 1607) gave New England its name after he mapped the area from Penobscot Bay, in present-day Maine, to Cape Cod in 1614.

During the early 1600s, unrest was growing in England. The Church of England had become very powerful and forbade people to practice other religions. Some people opposed to the Church of England became known as Separatists, and some of them decided to leave.

On September 16, 1620, a group of 102 Separatists (now known as Pilgrims) and other English people set sail for America aboard a ship named the *Mayflower*. The two-month sea journey was horrid. The Pilgrims had been granted territory in Virginia, but the Mayflower strayed off course, and the newcomers came ashore at Cape Cod. After attempts to reach a destination in New York failed, they decided to stay near where they first landed. They wrote an agreement called the Mayflower Compact. In it, they promised to govern themselves and to make only fair and just laws "for ye generall good of ye Colonie."

The first Pilgrim settlement was a coastal village they called Plimoth (spelled Plymouth today). The Pilgrims knew that a cold winter would soon be upon them, so they quickly built homes using poles and grasses. Wild animals lurked in the woods, and the Native people made the Pilgrims uneasy. Yet they were pleasantly surprised to find fields ready for planting. It gave them hope for spring.

The Wampanoag tribe and their chief, Massasoit, watched the newcomers carefully. Finally, the chief sent a messenger named Samoset, who arrived at Plymouth and said simply, "Welcome, English." (Samoset had probably learned some of the language from

In this engraving, the Pilgrims meet Chief Massasoit and other Wampanoags for the first time.

The Native People

Many people lived in Massachusetts before the first European settlers arrived. These people were the Natives of Massachusetts. In fact, the name Massachusetts comes from the Algonquin word Massachuset, which means, "near the range of hills." The eastern section of the state, including the Atlantic coastal portions of the land, were settled by the Wampanoag people, which included the Massachusett, the Nantucket, the Nauset, the Pennacook, the Pocasset, and the Pokanoket. The central portion of the state was settled by the Mohegan (including the Nipmuc and Pequot tribes). The Mohican tribe, as well as the Pocumtuc, were located in the western portion of what is now Massachusetts.

Most of the Native tribes of the Massachusetts region raised their own food through farming. Corn, squash, and beans were common crops. The men also hunted deer, turkeys, and small game to supplement their meals. The people that lived on the ocean's coast fished as well. Most of the Native people of Massachusetts lived in wigwams, small rounded houses constructed with wooden frames covered with birchbarks. Another name for wigwam was wetu, the Wampanoag term for "house."

As the Europeans settled in the Massachusetts colony, they made contact with more local tribes in an attempt to convert the Natives to Christianity. This contact had deadly consequences, as the Europeans introduced diseases that the Natives had never been exposed to before, and these illnesses wiped out significant portions of their population. In order to survive, many of the descimated tribes merged together, but these combinations led to a loss of tribal distinctions. Traditions were lost over time, and distinct languages merged into a single way of speaking.

Today there are two federally recognized Native tribes in Massachusetts—the Mashpee Wampanoag Indian Tribal Council and the Wampanoag Tribe of Gay Head (Aquinnah) of Massachusetts. The state itself recognizes the Nipmuc Nation as well.

Spotlight on the Wampanoag

"Wampanoag" means "easterners." In the 1600s, there were more than 10,000 Wampanoag people in dozens of villages along the coast of Massachusetts, including what is now Cape Cod and the islands of Nantucket and Martha's Vineyard. Today a few thousand Wampanoag people live in New England. There is a reservation for the tribe on Martha's Vineyard.

A depiction of the settlers of the Plymouth Colony sharing a harvest Thanksgiving meal with the local Wampanoag tribe.

Organization: The Wampanoag were organized into a **confederation**. The leader was called a *sachem*, who led over other lower-level sachems within the organization. Both women and men could be sachems.

Clothing: The Wampanoag wore breechcloths, which were made from deerskin. Women often wore deerskin skirts tied with thin belts. Both men and women wore leggings to protect their legs. Women's leggings were made of deerskin and tied at the knee. Men's leggings were longer, and they were tied at the waist.

Children: Young Wampanoag boys learned to gather, hunt, and fish from their parents. Young girls learned how to make clothing, plant crops, and collect food. Both girls and boys were taught how to work together as a community. They also learned from their elders through the stories that they told.

Games: One game the Wampanoag played was called "the bowl game" or "hubbub." It consisted of a wooden bowl and flat, marked playing pieces. One side of these pieces was dark and the other side was light. The players bounced the playing pieces by bumping the bowl. They kept score using sticks that were passed back and forth, depending on who won each toss. As the players bounced the pieces, they said "hub, hub, hub."

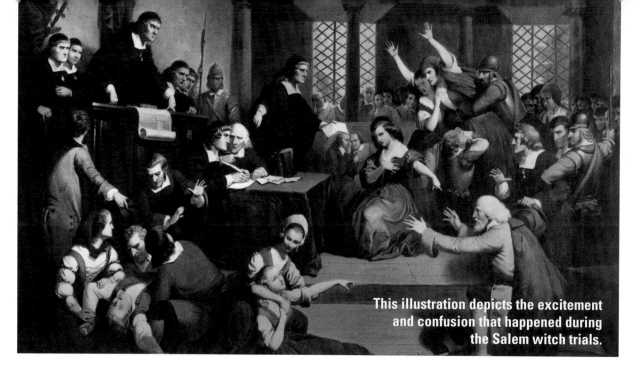

This illustration depicts the excitement and confusion that happened during the Salem witch trials.

Englishmen who came to fish off the coast of what is now northern New England and Canada.) The Pilgrims were excited to find someone who spoke their language and eagerly began to ask him questions. They wondered why there were fields ready for planting but no people in the area. Samoset told them the tilled fields belonged to the Patuxets, a tribe whose members had all died from disease. After Samoset brought his report back to Massasoit, the chief and his attendants visited Plymouth. Though there was little trust between the two groups, the Wampanoags and the Pilgrims signed the first peace treaty between Europeans and Native Americans. It lasted for more than 50 years.

One member of Chief Masassoit's party was a man named Tisquantum, or Squanto. He was the last remaining Patuxet. He spoke English because he had once lived in England as a slave. Squanto wanted to live on his **ancestors**' land and decided to help the Pilgrims. He taught them how to grow corn, where to hunt and fish, and which berries and nuts were good to eat. Thanks to Squanto, the Pilgrims were able to survive their first year in the new land and harvest a crop. For three days after the harvest, the Pilgrims and Massasoit's tribe celebrated an English feast called Harvest Home, which Americans now call Thanksgiving. In the following years, the Pilgrims' colony grew in size as more people came from England and several new towns were established.

The Massachusetts Bay Colony

In 1628, the first members of another religious group—the Puritans—arrived in the area. They joined an existing small settlement that was later named Salem. In 1630, a much larger group of Puritans arrived and soon settled nearby in what is now Boston to establish the Massachusetts Bay Colony.

The Puritans built small villages surrounding a section of open land called a commons. They farmed nearby fields in warm weather and made useful things, such as furniture, farm tools, horse harnesses, and clothing, in winter. The Puritans were stern people who believed in simple living and hard work.

New settlers continued to arrive from England, and the Massachusetts settlements grew. In 1691, England combined the Plymouth and Massachusetts Bay colonies into the single colony of Massachusetts.

The Dark Days

In many ways, life was difficult in seventeenth-century Massachusetts. The Puritans were powerful and often forced their beliefs on others. Puritan farmers and Native Americans fought bitterly over land. Many colony members did not trust one another. In 1692, when two girls in Salem fell sick seemingly without cause, the so-called Dark Days began. The girls fainted, had **seizures**, and slept little. A doctor declared them bewitched, a condition punishable by hanging. The girls blamed a slave named Tituba, saying, "She afflicts me! She comes to me at night and torments me! She's a witch!"

Soon, people all over Salem were accusing each other of witchcraft. Most of the accused were unmarried or widowed women who owned farmland. Many historians think that the accusers wanted the women's property. A court was set up to hear the witchcraft cases. In less than a year, more than 150 people were sent to prison. By the time the "Witchcraft Court" was shut down, 19 people had been hanged and one person had been pressed to death under heavy stones.

The Salem witchcraft trials marked a troubled time in Massachusetts's history, as did the struggle over land between the Native Americans and the English colonists. In 1675, Massasoit's son, Metacom, or King Philip as he was called by English settlers, declared war after the colonisists executed three tribesman. After two years of brutal fighting, King Philip was killed in battle. Many of his Native American supporters fled to Canada or westward. Others stayed and adopted English ways.

Making a Quill Pen and Ink

During the 1600s and 1700s, people in Massachusetts used quill pens and ink to write letters and other important documents. Quill pens were made with feathers from geese, swans, turkeys, and even crows. Follow these directions to make your own quill pen and ink.

What You Need

1/2 cup (75 grams) ripe berries

Strainer

Bowl

Wooden spoon

1/2 teaspoon (2.5 milliliters) vinegar

1/2 teaspoon (2.5 ml) salt

Baby food jar, empty and clean

Hollow feather from a craft store

Safety scissors

What To Do

To make the ink:

- Fill the strainer with the berries, and hold it over a bowl.

- Using the rounded back of a wooden spoon, crush the berries against the strainer so that the berry juice strains into the bowl.

- Keep adding berries until most of their juice has been strained out.

- Add the salt and vinegar to the berry juice (If the berry ink is too thick, add some water.)

- Store ink in baby food jar.

To make the quill:

- Use the scissors to cut the end of the feather at a slant so there is a pointy tip.

- Cut a vertical slit up into the tip of the pen.

- Dip the pen into the ink and have fun writing on your paper!

Wars and Taxes

King Philip's War, as it was called, was not the only land conflict the colonists—or the English—faced in America. Fur traders and settlers from France had also come to eastern North America. In the 1600s and 1700s, France and Great Britain fought several wars for control of eastern North America and its valuable natural resources. The French and Indian War (1754–1763) was the largest of these conflicts. Great Britain won the war, but the victory came at a great price. The British government had borrowed a great deal of money to pay for the war, and it needed to keep British troops in North America.

To help raise money to pay off the country's debt, King George III and the British Parliament began imposing new taxes on the colonies. The king was also eager to regain control over colonial governments that had been acting more and more independently while Britain was distracted by its wars. The British government wanted its American colonies to trade only with Britain, but many people in Massachusetts wanted to be free to trade with other countries too.

Several new taxes and other actions by the British government, starting in 1763, angered the colonists. When the first of the Townshend Acts was passed in 1767, many colonists had had enough. The Townshend Acts put new taxes on many kinds of imported goods. Many colonists did not feel they should have to pay taxes imposed by a government in which they had no voice. Colonists who opposed the actions of the British government became known as patriots. Their battle cry became, "No taxation without representation!"

The seeds for independence had been sown, and they flowered first in Massachusetts. On March 5, 1770, British soldiers opened fire on colonial protesters in an attack later known as the Boston Massacre. Five people were killed. Later, to oppose the British government's tax on tea, a group of colonists known as the Sons of Liberty organized a protest called the Boston Tea Party. One night in 1773, the protesters sneaked aboard a ship full of English tea in Boston Harbor and threw the tea overboard. In 1774, the British government passed a series of laws that became known in the colonies as the Intolerable Acts. One of the measures was to close the port of Boston.

On December 16, 1773, colonists dumped 342 containers of tea into Boston Harbor to protest British taxation.

Soon British soldiers, or "regulars," wearing red coats were everywhere. Farmers put down their plows for guns. They called themselves minutemen because it was said they could prepare for battle in just one minute. When British soldiers planned to march on the towns of Lexington and Concord (outside Boston) to capture patriot leaders and seize weapons, a group of patriots discovered their plan. Boston silversmith Paul Revere secretly rowed across the Charles River, and he and two other men then journeyed on horseback through the countryside to warn the minutemen that the British were coming.

An American Revolution

On April 19, 1775, minutemen and British regulars confronted each other at Lexington. It is not known for certain who fired the first shot—what poet Ralph Waldo Emerson later called "the shot heard 'round the world"—but the first fighting of the American Revolution took place at Lexington that day. From Lexington, the British went on to Concord, where they battled again with minutemen. As the British retreated back to Boston, colonial forces repeatedly shot at them. At the end of the day's fighting, some 250 British soldiers were dead or wounded, and about 90 Americans had been killed or injured. The military consequences were not great, but the outcome gave the colonists hope. They had managed to embarrass the better equipped, better trained—and more respected—British army.

After the battles of Lexington and Concord, the British soldiers stayed in Boston, and reinforcements arrived in May. In June, American forces were sent to Charlestown Peninsula, across the Charles River from Boston, to occupy Bunker Hill. They ended up building fortifications on nearby Breed's Hill. British soldiers tried to storm the fortifications and were pushed back twice, suffering heavy losses. The American forces, low on **ammunition**, fled when the British regulars made their third charge.

More than 1,000 British troops and about 400 Americans were killed or wounded during the Battle of Bunker Hill. Although the colonists had been pushed back, they still encircled the British in Boston. Months later, in March 1776, General George Washington took control of colonial troops around Boston. His forces occupied and put cannons on Dorchester Heights, a line of hills south of Boston that overlooked the city. British general William Howe soon realized he was in the middle of enemy territory occupying a city that he could not defend. On March 17, 1776, the British army left Boston for good.

British military forces reach the top of Breed's Hill, where they clash with colonial troops during the Battle of Bunker Hill in 1775.

10 KEY CITIES

Boston

Worcester

Cambridge

1. Boston: population 617,594

Boston, the state capital, is the largest city in New England. One of the oldest cities in America, it is home to several important events surrounding the American Revolution, such as the Boston Massacre and the Boston Tea Party.

2. Worcester: population 181,045

Located west of Boston, Worcester is pronounced "WOO-STER." The city is known for its many ethnic neighborhoods, including Little Italy, Union Hill, and Kelly Square. There is also a large art and music scene there.

3. Springfield: population 153,060

Springfield, in Southwest Massachusetts, is nicknamed the "City of Firsts." The city was the home of the first American dictionary, the first basketball game, the discovery of vulcanized rubber, and more.

4. Lowell: population 106,519

Located in Northeast Massachusetts, Lowell was a planned industrial city that was founded in the 1820s. Today, the city has a vibrant art scene, and it is one of the safest cities in the state.

5. Cambridge: population 105,162

Cambridge, outside of Boston, is known for being the home of two of the most respected universities in the United States. Harvard University and the Massachusetts Institute of Technology are both located there.

MASSACHUSETTS

6. New Bedford: population 95,072

New Bedford, in Southeast Massachusetts, is known as the "Whaling City" because it was one of the most important whaling ports of the nineteenth century. In 1841, Herman Melville set out from New Bedford on a whaling ship. His experience inspired him to write *Moby Dick*.

7. Brockton: population 93,810

Located south of Boston, Brockton is nicknamed the "City of Champions" because it was the home of two famous and successful boxers, Rocky Marciano and Marvin Hagler. The city was named one of the United States' "100 Best Communities for Young People" in 2011.

8. Quincy: population 92,271

Known as the "City of Presidents," Quincy was the home of two U.S. Presidents, John Adams and John Quincy Adams. Not far from Boston, Quincy has restaurants, golf courses, and miles of coastline to enjoy.

9. Lynn: population 90,329

Lynn is a manufacturing and commercial community north of Boston. Places of interest include Lynn Woods Reservation, where there is rumored to be pirate treasure buried, Spring Pond, and Fraser Field.

10. Fall River: population 88,857

This city located near New Bedford is known for its large Portuguese-American population and Battleship Cove, the world's largest collection of WWII naval vessels. Visitors also enjoy the city's museums and waterfront.

New Bedford

Brockton

Lynn

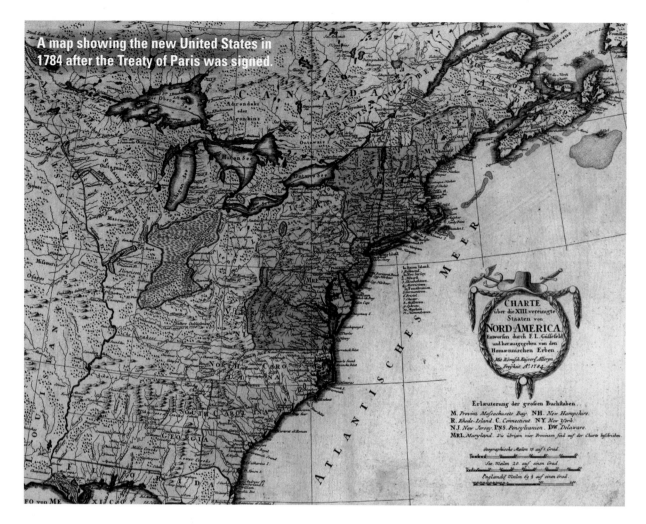

A map showing the new United States in 1784 after the Treaty of Paris was signed.

Declaring Independence

A few months later, on July 4, 1776, the Continental Congress—representatives of all the colonies meeting in Philadelphia—adopted the Declaration of Independence. Of course, declaring independence does not make it so. For the next seven years, the colonists continued to battle British soldiers throughout the Thirteen Colonies. By the time the Treaty of Paris ended the war in 1783, with Great Britain recognizing American independence, it is estimated that more than 25,000 American soldiers had died for the cause.

No Ordinary Rock

According to legend, Plymouth Rock is where the Pilgrims first landed in 1620. Today, the rock is housed in Massachusetts's smallest state park, Pilgrim Memorial State Park. Every year about 1,000,000 tourists come to Plymouth Rock.

In Massachusetts, John Adams and other leaders wrote a constitution for the Commonwealth of Massachusetts. (The first draft was called a Constitution for the State of Massachusetts, but people rejected it.) The document included rules for a new government that was based on **democracy** and citizens' rights—which did not include rights for women and slaves. It was a model for the U.S. Constitution and the Bill of Rights. In 1788, Massachusetts became the sixth state to ratify the U.S. Constitution.

Revolutionary Ideas

In the nineteenth century, Massachusetts played a major role in another revolution—the Industrial Revolution. There had been manufacturing in Massachusetts since the mid–1600s, but the state did not become a powerhouse in the industry until about 200 years later. In 1814, a Massachusetts resident named Francis Cabot Lowell built a loom in Waltham that ran by waterpower. A loom is a device that weaves thread into cloth. Lowell had visited a cotton mill in England, where he closely examined the workings of a power loom. Before he built his first mill with a water-powered loom, American looms

The young women who worked in Lowell's textile factories in the 1850s were known as Lowell Mill Girls.

This illustration shows smoke coming from the chimney of the Pontoosuc Woollen Manufacturing Company factory in Pittsfield.

were operated by hand. A water-powered loom can weave cloth much more quickly than a hand-operated one. Another one of Lowell's mills transformed the town of Lowell into the nation's first major manufacturing city. The Industrial Revolution had come to Massachusetts.

Cities such as Lawrence, Fall River, and New Bedford soon had large factories for making textiles (cloth), taking advantage of the waterpower in the state's rivers. By the end of the nineteenth century, Massachusetts produced more than a third of the nation's wool and cotton cloth. In Dalton, the Crane Paper Company produced the special paper used to make the nation's money. Factories in Lynn, Worcester, and Marlborough made shoes and boots for the entire country. Many factory employees were women and children who worked long hours in difficult conditions for very little pay.

Wars and Peace

Industrialized states in the North contrasted with those in the South, where agriculture was the main industry. Another issue, slavery, eventually divided the two regions even further. On the **plantations** of the South, most of the hard labor was done by African-American slaves.

Massachusetts was the first slaveholding New England colony, but it had abolished (ended) slavery by 1783. Other Northern states subsequently abolished slavery as well. Like other Northern states, Massachusetts had an abolitionist (or antislavery) movement, dedicated to ending slavery nationwide. Many people say the movement began in 1831, when William Lloyd Garrison first published his antislavery

This engraving depicts an anti-slavery meeting on Boston Common.

CRADLE OF LIBERTY

The 54th Massachusetts Regiment was one of the first African-American regiments in the United States.

newspaper, the *Liberator*, in Boston. Eventually, the differences between North and South led eleven Southern states to secede (withdraw) from the United States. The Civil War (1861–1865) was fought to keep the nation together.

When the Civil War broke out, Massachusetts quickly answered President Abraham Lincoln's call to arms. The state sent the first troops into battle. Military units from Massachusetts included the 54th Massachusetts Regiment, one of the first African-American regiments in the country. Those who remained at home went to work in factories making guns, ammunition, ships, tents, blankets, and bandages. After the South was defeated and the Civil War ended, the Thirteenth Amendment to the U.S. Constitution abolished slavery throughout the United States.

In the 1840s, thousands of immigrants came to Massachusetts to escape a severe **famine** in Ireland. In the later decades of the nineteenth century, people from many different countries poured into Massachusetts looking for work. **Immigrants** from France,

Italy, Poland, Ireland, Portugal, Germany, and Greece joined immigrants from Finland, Latvia, Lithuania, and Turkey in seeking a better life in the commonwealth. Many of these workers had valuable skills, and because of them, Massachusetts prospered. This era of progress, known as the Industrial Age, lasted through the outbreak of World War I.

When America entered World War I in 1917, many Massachusetts citizens enlisted to fight for their country. Others stayed at home, building guns and ships and manufacturing other supplies. After the war ended, telephones, automobiles, electricity, and other new conveniences rapidly improved daily life.

As the men of Massachusetts left to fight in World War I, the state's women stepped up to fill their roles at home.

Then, in 1929, the stock market crashed and everything changed. During the period known as the Great Depression, people lost their jobs, businesses closed, and banks failed. Few people escaped hardship. The federal government took many steps to strengthen the economy, and in time, things began to turn around. When World War II broke out in Europe in 1939, once again, Massachusetts's skilled workers were needed. By 1941, the United States had entered the war, and Massachusetts's factories were busy producing wartime goods.

After the war, Massachusetts continued to grow. Boston became an international trading city. Workers found new jobs in medicine and technology. Scientists and researchers made exciting discoveries at colleges and universities and in hospital laboratories throughout the state. New immigrants from Asia, Latin America, and the Caribbean settled in Massachusetts and added to the rich mix of cultures and ideas. Over the years, people in Massachusetts have taken great pride in their state's leading place in the country and in the world.

During World War II, Massachusetts's factories, such as this General Electric plant, manufactured parts for U.S. warships.

10 KEY DATES IN STATE HISTORY

1. 1500s

Algonquians, including the Nipmuc, Nauset, Patuxet, and Wampanoag tribes, live in the region.

2. 1614

English captain John Smith maps the coast of northern New England from Maine to Cape Cod.

3. December, 1620

The Pilgrims settle in Plymouth. The colony lasts until 1691. At its peak, Plymouth occupies most of Southeast Massachusetts.

4. April 19, 1775

After tensions build up between the 13 colonies and Britain, the American Revolution begins with the Battles of Lexington and Concord. The war ends eight years later.

5. February 6, 1788

Massachusetts becomes the sixth state to ratify the U.S. Constitution during a time of economic unrest.

6. March 11, 1892

The first game of basketball is played at the YMCA in Springfield. Around 200 people are there to watch it.

7. November 8, 1960

John F. Kennedy of Brookline is elected U.S. President. Three years later he is assassinated.

8. October 27, 2004

The Boston Red Sox win baseball's World Series for the first time since 1918, ending what many thought was a curse on their team.

9. January 4, 2007

Deval Patrick, the first African-American governor of Massachusetts, takes office. He began his second term in 2011.

10. April 15, 2013

Two bombs explode near the finish line of the Boston Marathon, killing 3 and injuring hundreds. One suspect is killed and one is captured several days later.

Boston Red Sox fans walk outside of Fenway Park. Red Sox fans are known for being very passionate about their team.

The People

Massachusetts is filled with people who have come from, or whose ancestors have come from, all over the world. These people of diverse backgrounds bring their own traditions and learn about those of others. Together, they make Massachusetts an exciting and interesting place to live.

Massachusetts ranks 45th among the states in size, but as of 2013, it ranked fourteenth in population. Only two states—New Jersey and Rhode Island—have denser populations. (Population density refers to the number of people per square mile or square kilometer.) Today, almost half of all Bay Staters live in towns, cities, and suburbs within 50 miles (80 km) of Boston.

A Cultural Bean Pot

After the Native American population shrank, English settlers became the most powerful group in Massachusetts. For centuries, the families who traced their beginnings in America to the *Mayflower*, such as the Cabot, Lodge, Adams, Emerson, and Lowell families, dominated the culture of the commonwealth. For the most part, this hardworking, reserved group of people, often called Yankees, represented the Massachusetts way of life to the world.

The St. Patrick's Day Parade in South Boston always draws a huge crowd.

Then, in the 1840s, Irish immigrants came in great numbers to escape Ireland's potato famine. The Yankees felt threatened by the Irish immigrants and tried to keep them from going to public events. They even posted "No Irish Need Apply" signs to keep the new arrivals from getting jobs. Today, however, Irish Americans are the state's largest ethnic group and are very active in the state's politics, society, and trade.

After the Irish came ashore, people from Germany, Russia, Poland, Portugal, Italy, Greece, and French Canada immigrated to Massachusetts. These eager newcomers settled in the many mill and factory towns and began building communities.

After the European cultures created a flavorful blend of traditions, a new ingredient was added. Since the 1970s, immigrants from the Caribbean and Asia have settled in Lowell and other cities. Often, children playing in neighborhood parks speak English to one another while at night they speak Khmer (the language of Cambodia) or Spanish to family members at home. Lowell's Cambodian community is the second largest in the nation.

Many of Boston's neighborhoods have a lively ethnic and cultural atmosphere. Its oldest neighborhood, the North End, has a rich immigrant history. Its narrow streets were laid out in the 1600s along the city's **wharves**. When immigrants stepped off their ships, they found it easy to move into the buildings nearby. English, Polish, Russian, Jewish, Portuguese, Irish, and Italian immigrants all made homes in this historic community. Today, the neighborhood is mostly Italian. Hispanics from the Dominican Republic, Puerto Rico, Cuba, and many other Spanish-speaking areas have contributed to the blend of cultures in neighborhoods south of Boston.

Another lively neighborhood full of shops, businesses, and restaurants is Chinatown. Many people of Chinese, Japanese, Korean, Cambodian, and Vietnamese descent live and work there. "I think we should call it Asian Town," said one community leader.

People have come to live in Massachusetts for many reasons, but they all have come hoping for a fresh start. As one lifelong resident asked, "Why would anyone want to be anywhere else?"

A girl tries on a mask at the Quincy Lunar New Year Festival, which celebrates the Chinese New Year.

10 KEY PEOPLE

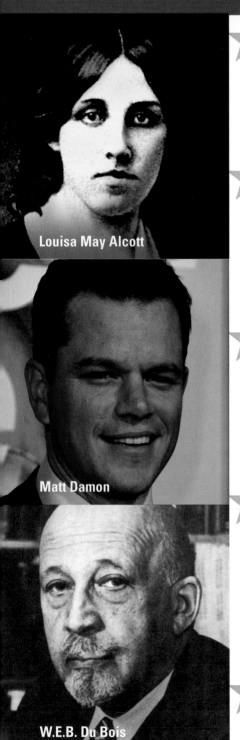

Louisa May Alcott

Matt Damon

W.E.B. Du Bois

1. Louisa May Alcott

Louisa May Alcott was born in Pennsylvania in 1832 but lived most of her life in Boston and Concord. She published her first book in 1854. Alcott's most famous book, *Little Women*, remains an American classic.

2. Michael Carter-Williams

Michael Carter-Williams was born in Hamilton in 1991. He played basketball in high school, during which he averaged 23 points per game. Carter-Williams spent two years playing at Syracuse University before being drafted by the NBA's Philadelphia 76ers.

3. Matt Damon

Actor Matt Damon was born in 1970 in Cambridge. He studied English at Harvard before pursuing a film career. Damon has starred in many movies, including *Good Will Hunting*, which he cowrote with friend Ben Affleck. They won the Academy Award for Best Original Screenplay for the film in 1997.

4. W.E.B. Du Bois

William Edward Burghardt Du Bois was born in Great Barrington in 1868. In 1895, he became the first African American to earn a doctoral degree from Harvard. Du Bois cofounded the NAACP (National Association for the Advancement of Colored People) and wrote more than 20 books.

5. Theodor Geisel (Dr. Seuss)

Born in Springfield, Geisel, who called himself Dr. Seuss, wrote and illustrated some of the most clever, entertaining children's books ever written, including *Green Eggs and Ham*.

MASSACHUSETTS

6. Mindy Kaling

Vera Mindy Chokalingam (Kaling) was born in Cambridge in 1979. In college, Kaling was part of a comedy group, and she wrote for the college's humor magazine. She appeared in several movies before becoming a writer for the hit show *The Office*, in which she later starred.

Mindy Kaling

Lucy Stone

7. Nancy Kerrigan

Born in Woburn in 1969, Nancy Kerrigan started figure skating at an early age. She won a bronze medal at the 1992 Winter Olympics. In January 1994, Kerrigan was attacked by the ex-husband of fellow skater Tonya Harding. Despite her knee injury, Kerrigan won the silver medal at the Olympics that year.

8. Amy Poehler

Born in Newton in 1971, Amy Poehler moved to Chicago after college and joined the comedy groups Second City and the Upright Citizens' Brigade. Poehler's big break came when she was hired as a performer on *Saturday Night Live*. Poehler then went on to star in *Parks and Recreation*.

9. Lucy Stone

Lucy Stone was born in 1818 in West Brookfield. In 1847, she became one of the first Massachusetts women to earn a college degree. Stone organized the first convention on women's rights in Worcester in 1850.

10. Eli Whitney

Born in 1765 in Westboro, Eli Whitney invented the cotton gin, a machine that simplified the process of separating fiber from cotton seeds. The cotton gin was one of the most important inventions in history.

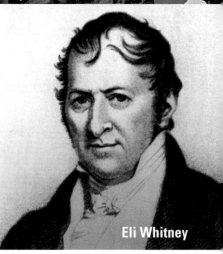

Eli Whitney

Who Massachusetters Are

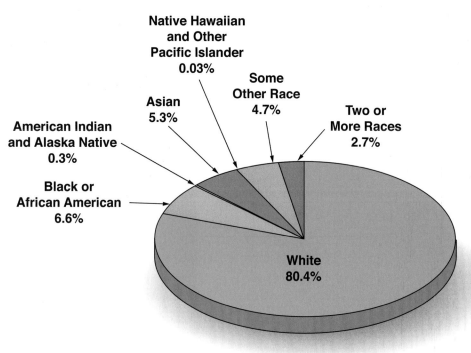

Native Hawaiian and Other Pacific Islander 0.03%

Some Other Race 4.7%

Asian 5.3%

American Indian and Alaska Native 0.3%

Two or More Races 2.7%

Black or African American 6.6%

White 80.4%

Total Population 6,547,629

Hispanic or Latino (of any race):
- 627,654 people (9.6%)

Note: The pie chart shows the racial breakdown of the state's population based on the categories used by the U.S. Bureau of the Census. The Census Bureau reports information for Hispanics or Latinos separately, since they may be of any race. Percentages in the pie chart may not add to 100 because of rounding.

Source: U.S. Bureau of the Census, 2010 Census

The Commonwealth of Learning

Higher education has been the soul of Massachusetts since the 1600s. Harvard University, founded in 1636, was the first institution of higher learning in what would become the United States. Later, in the nineteenth century, many other major colleges and universities were established in Massachusetts. In or near the capital city are Boston University, Brandeis University, Northeastern University, Boston College, and the Massachusetts Institute of Technology (MIT). Farther west are Williams College, Clark University, Amherst College, the University of Massachusetts, and the Worcester Polytechnic Institute. Women's colleges such as Radcliffe (now part of Harvard), Smith, Mount Holyoke, and Wellesley were founded in the late nineteenth century. Because many Massachusetts residents are so well educated, the Bay State has long been at the leading edge of ideas and achievements.

Massachusetts was the first state in the nation to require all children to attend public school, but not all schools were equal. Throughout most of the country's history, many schools in the United States were **segregated**. White children and black children went to different schools.

In many Southern states, laws and government policies established totally separate school systems for white children and black children. In many states, including Massachusetts, this was not the case. However, African-American families tended to live in different neighborhoods, so their children went to different schools. The schools for African-American children often had inferior facilities and out-of-date textbooks. In 1954, in a case called *Brown v. Board of Education of Topeka, Kansas*, the U.S. Supreme Court ruled that segregated schools violated the U.S. Constitution. Still, many states were slow to integrate their school systems.

In 1965, more than ten years after the Brown ruling, Boston schools were still largely segregated, and schools in black neighborhoods tended to be inferior to those in white areas of the city. With the help of the NAACP, black parents complained to the Boston School **Committee**. However, Louise Hicks, the committee chair, claimed the black schools were not inferior. "A racially imbalanced school," she said, "is not educationally harmful."

After years of trying to change the situation, black parents in Boston finally took their case to court. In 1974, a federal district court judge ordered the schools to integrate. To

Harvard University, founded in Cambridge in 1636 as Harvard College, is one of the most respected educational institutions in the world.

African-American students travel under police escort in 1974 during Boston's school integration crisis.

achieve a balance of black students and white students, children were bused to schools in different parts of the city. Many white people opposed busing. In September, buses carrying black students in South Boston were met by angry mobs throwing rocks. Some white parents even pulled their children out of school. The resistance to busing and the violent behavior continued for years. The situation finally settled down after Hicks was replaced as committee chair and a black person was elected to the committee.

Almost a decade before forced busing in Boston, the voluntary busing METCO (Metropolitan **Council** for Educational Opportunity) program began sending inner-city students to suburban schools. More than 3,000 students currently participate in the program. More than five times that number are on a waiting list, hoping they will get the chance to earn a quality education. Some people argue that instead of spending money on busing, the government should invest in improving inner-city schools. Others fear that this would eventually lead back to fully segregated schools. Unlike 40 years ago, however, advocates on both sides are focused on the welfare of the children.

The opportunity for children to receive quality education is an important topic in Massachusetts.

10 KEY EVENTS

1. America's Hometown Thanksgiving

This celebration is held in Plymouth, where the first Thanksgiving took place, on the weekend before the holiday. It features concerts, a parade, food, and a historic village. More than 250,000 people attend the celebration each year.

2. Boston Marathon and Patriots' Day

On the third Monday in April, citizens gather in Boston and nearby towns to watch reenactments of Paul Revere's ride and the battles of Lexington and Concord. Later, they line the streets to cheer on thousands of runners in the world's oldest annual marathon.

3. Boston Pops Fireworks Spectacular

On July 4, the Boston Pops Orchestra gives a rousing patriotic concert along the banks of the Charles River under a sky full of fireworks to celebrate Independence Day. More than 500,000 people attend every year, and it is televised on national TV.

4. Chinese New Year

On the lunar New Year, which falls in January or February, thousands of people gather in Boston's Chinatown to watch costumed lion dances and fireworks. Following tradition, many decorate their doorways in red and give children gifts of money in red and gold envelopes.

5. Dragon Boat Festival

In June, Asian Americans sponsor the Charles River Dragon Boat Festival in Boston. The longest-running dragon boat festival in North America includes dancing, music, drumming, food, and races featuring beautifully carved wooden boats.

Boston Marathon

Boston Pops Fireworks

Chinese New Year

MASSACHUSETTS

6. First Night

One of the country's largest New Year's Eve celebrations is held in Boston. The celebration of community and the arts includes theater, music, dance, food, and fireworks.

7. Head of the Charles Regatta

In October, more than 7,500 competitors from around the world compete in around 55 different racing events on Boston's Charles River. It is the world's largest two-day rowing event. The Regatta attracts more than 300,000 people each year.

8. Mashpee Wampanoag Powwow

In July, visitors are invited to Mashpee, on Cape Cod, where Wampanoags host their annual powwow. Tribal members perform traditional dances, songs, drumming, and storytelling. They also serve a feast of lobster, quahogs (clams), strawberries, and corn bread.

9. St. Patrick's Day Parade

Around 24 percent of Boston's residents are Irish, and the city's St. Patrick's Day Parade is one of the largest parades in the United States. The parade attracts more than 850,000 people each year. It includes floats, bagpipers, and marching bands.

10. The Big "E" [Eastern States Exposition]

New England's largest fair is held every September in West Springfield. More than 1,000,000 visitors enjoy agricultural events, arts and crafts, horse shows, farm animal and pet competitions, and concerts.

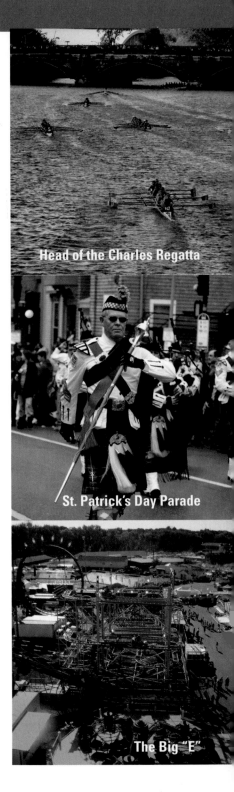

Head of the Charles Regatta

St. Patrick's Day Parade

The Big "E"

The Massachusetts State House is located on Beacon Hill across from the Boston Common.

How the Government Works

O n February 6, 1788, Massachusetts became the sixth state to ratify the U.S. Constitution. Its state constitution, called the Constitution of the Commonwealth of Massachusetts, is even older than the national government's. Adopted in 1780, it is the oldest state constitution still in use. Many amendments have been added, but the document that sets out how the state government operates has not been fundamentally changed in more than 200 years.

The elegant State House in Boston is the center of Massachusetts government. However, that is not the only place to find the government of Massachusetts at work. As the former speaker of the U.S. House of Representatives, Massachusetts congressman Thomas P. "Tip" O'Neill, Jr., once said, "All politics is local." The government of Massachusetts starts with every citizen. Anyone, of any age, can propose a law, and any U.S. citizen 18 or older who lives in Massachusetts can register to vote in local, state, and federal elections.

There are three levels of government in Massachusetts: city or town; county; and state. There are 14 counties, which are run by county commissioners. As in other New England states, county government is not very strong and has no authority to tax citizens. City dwellers elect mayors and city councilmembers to govern. Towns elect selectmen. Citizens and their elected officials regularly come together to discuss issues at town

Voters go to the polls on Election Day in Boston.

The Road to the White House

Five U.S. presidents have come from Massachusetts. John Adams was the nation's first vice president and the second president; his son John Quincy was the sixth president. Massachusetts Governor Calvin Coolidge was elected vice president in 1920 and became president upon the death of president Warren Harding. John F. Kennedy, from Brookline, was elected in 1960. Massachusetts is also the birthplace of George H. W. Bush, who was elected president in 1988.

meetings, a tradition dating to colonial times. People can also write to their elected leaders to share concerns and opinions. At the highest level of state government, voters elect state senators and representatives, a governor, and other executive officeholders.

As of 2014, there were nine Massachusetts representatives in the U.S. House of Representatives. Like all states, Massachusetts has two U.S. Senators in Washington, D.C. Edward "Ted" Kennedy was the fourth-longest-serving U.S. Senator. He was first elected to represent Massachusetts in 1962 at the age of 30. His career in the Senate spanned four decades, until his death in

2009. In that time, he became one of the U.S. Senate's most influential members.

The United States has two major parties: the Democratic Party and the Republican Party. Ted Kennedy, who was known as "the lion of the Senate," was respected for his ability to "reach across the aisle." He worked well with Republicans as well as members of his own party.

After Kennedy's death, a special election in 2010 determined who would finish out his term in the U.S. Senate. Republican Scott Brown ran against Democrat Martha Coakley and won. Massachusetts had a Republican U.S. senator for the first time in more than three decades. Brown served one term.

Branches of Government

Executive

The governor, lieutenant governor, and other executive officers are elected to four-year terms. The governor, who is the head of state and commander-in-chief of the state's militia (army), prepares the state budget, suggests new laws, and appoints judges and other department heads. The governor also has the power to sign bills into law or veto (refuse to sign) them.

Among other things, Massachusetts courts help determine whether laws are constitutional. This hearing takes place at the Massachusetts Supreme Court in Boston.

An important part of a governor's job is signing bills into law. Here Governor Deval Patrick signs a reform bill.

Legislative

The state house of representatives and state senate make up Massachusetts' legislature, which is called the Massachusetts General Court. The senate has 40 members, and the house of representatives has 160. Senators and representatives are elected to two-year terms. Legislators propose and pass the laws that are ultimately sent to the governor for signature.

Judicial

The state has a system of courts made up of a supreme judicial court, a court of appeals, and many trial courts. The supreme judicial court is the highest court in the commonwealth. Most cases start in a trial court. If there is a disagreement with a trial court ruling, the case may be heard by a court of appeals. Cases may be further appealed to the supreme judicial court. This court tends to hear only cases that raise important legal questions, including whether a law follows or violates the state constitution.

How a Bill Becomes a Law

The commonwealth has more state symbols than most states. It has a state muffin (corn), a state historical rock (Plymouth), and even a state bean (navy, as the original Boston baked bean). The story of how one symbol, the state insect, was chosen shows how laws are passed in Massachusetts.

One day in 1974 at Kennedy Elementary School in Franklin, Massachusetts, second-grade teacher Palma Johnson told her class about official state symbols. Her students asked why there was a state tree, bird, and fish but no state insect. They decided the ladybug would make an excellent state symbol and that they should try to make it official. The students learned that anyone living in Massachusetts could ask to have a law passed. First they needed a special form called a petition, as well as a legislator to sign it. So the children wrote to their representative, who agreed to sign their petition.

After that, there was much work to do. First the petition had to become a bill. It was given an identification number—House Bill 5155—and sent to a committee, which discussed whether the legislators should vote on it. Johnson's students went to the State House in Boston to explain why the ladybug should be the official state insect. They told the legislators, "They're so beautiful with their shiny orange backs and bold black spots, and they can be found in everyone's backyard."

The committee agreed with the students and presented the bill to the entire house of representatives. The representatives needed to talk about the bill three times before they could vote on it. The class visited or wrote letters to members of the House, asking them to vote for the bill. After the three discussions, the representatives voted to make the ladybug the official state insect.

In order to become a law, the bill had to go to the senate. The children returned to the Massachusetts State House, this time to the senate chamber. They asked for and received the senators' votes. The bill was very nearly a law. It was then printed on special paper called parchment and delivered to the governor.

If the governor signed it, the bill would be a law. If the governor vetoed it, the bill would not be a law. The governor did sign the bill, and the ladybug became the official state insect of Massachusetts.

POLITICAL FIGURES
FROM MASSACHUSETTS

John F. Kennedy: U.S. President, 1961-1963

Born in Brookline in 1917, JFK became a member of the U.S. House of Representatives and the U.S. Senate. He was elected the 35th President of the United States in 1960. As president, Kennedy faced foreign crises in Cuba and Berlin. Sadly, Kennedy was assassinated while riding in a motorcade in Dallas, Texas, on November 22, 1963.

Jane Swift: Acting Governor of Massachusetts, 2001-2003

Born in North Adams in 1965, Jane Swift became a member of the Massachusetts Senate in 1991, where she served for six years. In 1998, Swift was elected lieutenant governor of the state, and in 2001 she became acting governor. Swift is the first woman ever to hold that position.

Setti Warren: Mayor of Newton, 2010-

Setti Warren was born in Newton in 1970. Warren was class president in high school and student body president in college. After serving in the Navy in Iraq, Warren became the first popularly-elected African-American mayor in Massachusetts in 2010. He was elected to a second term in 2013.

MASSACHUSETTS
YOU CAN MAKE A DIFFERENCE

Contacting Lawmakers

You can e-mail Massachusetts state legislators or look up their names, addresses, and telephone numbers at: **www.mass.gov/legis**

The Law of the Land

The state legislature has the power to make laws. The judicial system has a powerful role in how the state's laws are interpreted. The courts are responsible for deciding whether state laws are legal under the Massachusetts constitution. If a law does not agree with

Elizabeth Freeman

the constitution, the Supreme Judicial Court can declare that law unconstitutional. A famous case argued in Massachusetts in the late 1700s illustrates how this works. An enslaved woman named Elizabeth Freeman brought the case to court.

Freeman's owner, Colonel John Ashley, was very involved in Massachusetts politics and government. While serving her owner and his political friends at the table, Freeman listened carefully to their conversations. The men discussed many issues of the day, including the new Massachusetts constitution.

One day, the colonel's wife tried to beat Freeman's sister. Freeman was furious. She marched through cold, icy weather to the home of Theodore Sedgwick, a lawyer who she knew did not support slavery. Freeman asked why the new constitution did not protect her and her sister. Yet the men at Colonel Ashley's dinner table were always talking about all people being "born free and equal."

Sedgwick agreed to take Freeman's case before a judge, where he argued that the law permitting slavery was unconstitutional. The judge agreed, saying that the true meaning of the 1780 state constitution clearly was that "all men are born free and equal." The judge ruled that Elizabeth Freeman and her sister were free—and slavery in Massachusetts was soon abolished.

Men fish for cod on their boat in Massachusetts.

Making a Living

The economy of Massachusetts has changed a great deal over the past almost 400 years. When the area was first settled by people from England, colonists made their living off the land. In addition to foreign trade, the base of Massachusetts's economy was formed by fishing and farming. These industries have shrunk dramatically over the years, however. Less than one percent of the state's workforce is engaged in these industries today. Manufacturing became a major part of the state's economy in the 1800s after Francis Cabot Lowell built his power loom. But in recent decades, manufacturing has declined. After World War II, computers and technology took on new importance. This "new economy" continues to be at the core of Massachusetts's economy, as do the service and tourism industries.

Fishing and Farming

In the late 1700s and early 1800s, fishing and whaling contributed greatly to the state's pocketbook. When the New Bedford whaling boom reached its peak in 1857, more than 300 vessels were sailing out of the port. The fleet, worth more than $12 million, employed 10,000 men. By the early 1900s, however, the whaling industry in America was virtually dead. Today, whale populations off the coast of Massachusetts contribute to the state

A farmer harvests cranberries.

economy in a much more humane way. According to the World Wildlife Fund, the Bay State is one of the top 10 whale-watching spots in the world.

New England's fishing industry has always been tied to groundfishing—catching bottom-dwelling fish such as cod and haddock. The 1970s saw a decline in the industry due to overfishing and pollution. The state has made a comeback, however, and the economic impact of Massachusetts's fishing industry is one of the top in the country.

Although fewer Bay-Staters work in farming than any other industry, the Bay State is still home to thousands of farms. In 2011, the value of agricultural production—crop and livestock sales—was almost $489 million. In southeastern Massachusetts, farmers grow about 26 percent of the country's cranberry crop. The tart red berry is one of the few truly Native American fruits. Algonquian tribes used it for food and medicine and as a dye for blankets and rugs.

Manufacturing

After Lowell introduced his power loom in the 1800s, textile manufacturing contributed a great deal to the economy of Massachusetts. Factories in the state also turned out shoes, leather goods, paper, lumber for building, printed goods, ships, tools, and games. Most of the original factories have shut down, but new ones have taken their places. Around 10 percent of Bay Staters work in factories manufacturing electrical and industrial equipment, technical instruments, plastic products, paper and paper products, machinery, tools, and metal and rubber goods.

Scientists at the Massachusetts Institute of Technology (MIT) worked with the U.S. Navy in the 1940s on a project that led to the design of a high-speed digital computer. And, in 1971, the world's first email was sent from a computer in Cambridge. Now, Route 128—the highway that circles Boston, Lexington, and Cambridge—links technology companies and major universities. Together they develop products and ideas that benefit the entire world.

In this photo, a robot called Atlas is shown off during a demonstration day at MIT.

10 KEY INDUSTRIES

Apples

Cranberries

Horticulture

1. Apples

McIntosh, Cortland, Pippin, and New England Red Delicious are among the many varieties of apples grown in the state. Most of the more than 100 apple orchards are family farms.

2. Cranberries

Massachusetts is the second-largest cranberry-producing state, after Wisconsin. Farmers produce around 2 million barrels of this colorful fruit each year. Most cranberry farms are in the southeastern part of the state, where saltwater bogs and wetlands make for an ideal growing environment.

3. Fishing

Fishing is a regular part of coastal life in Massachusetts. From New Bedford to Newburyport, fishers catch haddock, cod, and halibut using gillnets, longlines, or dragging gear. Others harvest lobsters and scallops.

4. Green Energy

There are many environmentally-friendly energy companies in Massachusetts. They make solar panels, wind turbines, and laptop batteries. These things help reduce pollution and lower our dependence on non-renewable resources.

5. Horticulture

Growing fruits, vegetables, flowers, shrubs, and trees has long been a part of the Massachusetts economy. Landscape plants for home gardens and lawns are the major horticultural crop in the state. In 1852, a Concord horticulturist bred a grape from different native varieties. He called it the "grape for the millions." Today, Concord grapes are used in juices, jams, and sweeteners around the world.

MASSACHUSETTS

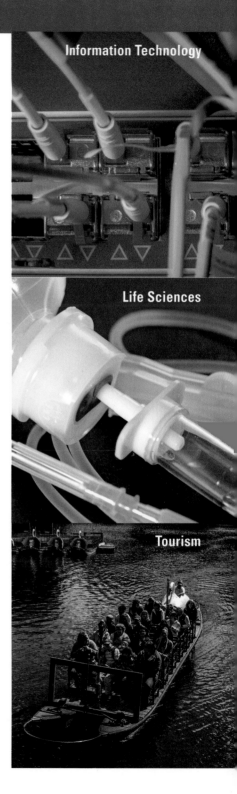

Information Technology

Life Sciences

Tourism

6. Information Technology

Information technology is technology involving the development, maintenance, and use of computer systems, software, and networks for the processing and distribution of data. The industry employs more than 170,000 people in over 3,000 companies throughout the state.

7. Life Sciences

From **pharmaceuticals** and medical devices to biotechnology, the life sciences are an important part of the state's economy. More than 80,000 jobs exist in the industry at universities, private companies, and medical centers.

8. Media

Film, music, publishing, and advertising are just some of the media-based fields that exist in Massachusetts. Most are located in Boston, which is often considered the second-largest city for media on the east coast, behind New York City.

9. Printing

The Boston-area economy has relied on printing, publishing, and bookbinding for more than a century. The very first printing press in the nation was used at the Cambridge Press, founded in 1639. James Franklin (Benjamin Franklin's brother) started the *New England Courant*, the first newspaper to include local news and opinion pieces, in Boston in 1721.

10. Tourism

The commonwealth's third-largest industry is tourism. It employs more than 126,000 people and generates more than $17.7 billion. Popular tourist destinations include Boston, Nantucket, Martha's Vineyard, and Cape Cod.

Recipe for Chocolate Chip Cookies

The chocolate chip cookie became Massachusetts's State Cookie in 1997 after a third grade class from Somerset proposed a bill. With the help of an adult, use this recipe to make chocolate chip cookies for you and your family!

What You Need

1 teaspoon (5 ml) baking soda

1 teaspoon (5 ml) salt

2 sticks butter, softened

3/4 cup (150 g) granulated sugar

3/4 cup (150 g) packed brown sugar

1 teaspoon (5 ml) vanilla extract

2 large eggs

12-ounce (340 g) package of chocolate chips

What to Do

- Preheat oven to 375° F (191° C).
- Combine flour, baking soda and salt in a small bowl.
- Stir butter, sugar, brown sugar, and vanilla extract in a large mixing bowl until creamy.
- Add eggs, one at a time, stirring well after each one.
- Gradually beat in flour mixture.
- Stir in chocolate chips.
- Use a spoon to drop dough onto an ungreased baking sheet.
- Bake for 9 to 11 minutes, or until golden brown.
- Cool on the baking sheet for 2 minutes.
- Transfer cookies to wire racks to cool completely.

Fun and Games

Massachusetts is home to some of the best-known teams in sports—and some of the most fanatical fans. The Boston Red Sox have been playing baseball in historic Fenway Park since 1912. After an 86-year drought (some people said the team was cursed), the Sox won the World Series in 2004 and again in 2007 and 2013. The Boston Celtics, the city's professional basketball team, has won 17 NBA titles over its storied history. That is more than any other team in the league. The New England Patriots call Foxborough's Gillette Stadium home. In 2005, the Pats became only the second team in NFL history to win three Super Bowls in four years. (They took home the trophy in Super Bowl XXXVI, XXXVIII, and XXXIX.)

Tourism

It is not surprising that a state as rich in history and natural attractions as Massachusetts has a thriving tourism industry. Every year, millions of people visit the Bay State to walk

Fans watch a Red Sox game from left field at Fenway Park.

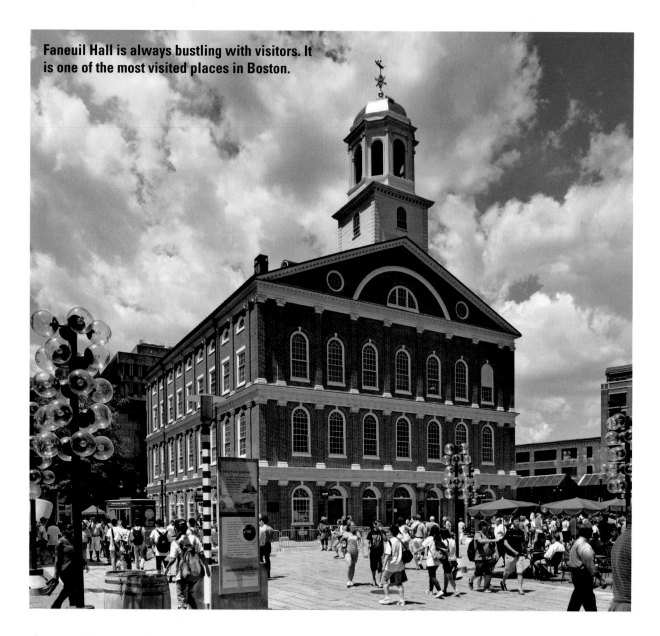

Faneuil Hall is always bustling with visitors. It is one of the most visited places in Boston.

the Freedom Trail, a 2.5-mile (4-km) walking path that includes sixteen historic sites. Stops along the trail include the site of the Boston Massacre, Paul Revere's house, and Faneuil Hall. Boston is sometimes called the Cradle of Liberty because of its association with revolutionary colonists, such as Samuel Adams.

Visitors to Massachusetts also enjoy fine dining, world-class museums, and cultural events. They experience the best Mother Nature has to offer in every season. The Berkshire Mountains are bursting with color during fall foliage time. In the winter, there is skiing, snowboarding, and other cold-weather activities. In summertime, people from all over the country flock to Cape Cod and beautiful Nantucket Island, where they might visit the quaint towns, go on a whale-watching trip, or relax on the beach.

On average, 18 million people from other states visit Massachusetts every year. They help provide jobs for the thousands of Bay Staters who work in hotels, restaurants, stores, tourist sites, and other service businesses. Massachusetts has a lot to offer. Residents and visitors will make sure this great state continues to thrive.

A family enjoys the impressive autumn colors of the Berkshires.

MASSACHUSETTS
STATE MAP

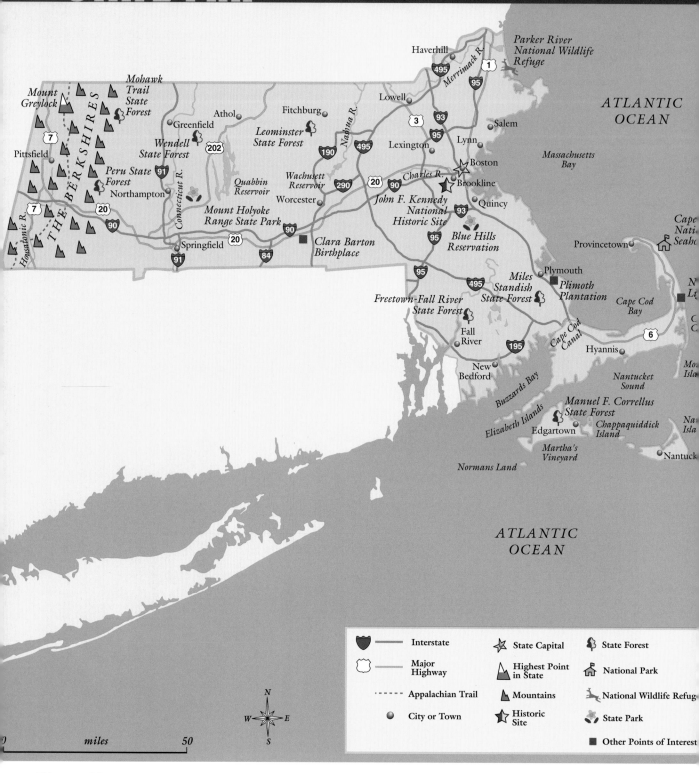

Haverhill

Parker River
National Wildlife
Refuge

Merrimack R.

495

1

95

ATLANTIC
OCEAN

Mohawk
Trail
State
Forest

Lowell

Mount
Greylock

Athol

Fitchburg

Leominster
State Forest

Greenfield

Nashua R.

3

93

95

Salem

Lexington

THE BERKSHIRES

Wendell
State Forest

202

190

495

Lynn

Pittsfield

7

Peru State
Forest

91

Quabbin
Reservoir

Wachusett
Reservoir

20

90

Charles R.

Boston

Brookline

Massachusetts
Bay

Connecticut R.

Northampton

290

Worcester

John F. Kennedy
National
Historic Site

Quincy

7

Housatonic R.

20

90

Mount Holyoke
Range State Park

20

John F. Kennedy
National
Historic Site

93

Cape
Nati
Seaho

Springfield

91

20

84

90

Clara Barton
Birthplace

95

Blue Hills
Reservation

Provincetown

Miles
Standish
State Forest

Plymouth

Plimoth
Plantation

N
Li

Freetown-Fall River
State Forest

495

Cape Cod
Bay

Fall
River

195

Cape Cod Canal

6

Hyannis

C
C

New
Bedford

Buzzards Bay

Nantucket
Sound

Mo
Isla

Elizabeth Islands

Manuel F. Correllus
State Forest

Chappaquiddick
Island

Na
Isla

Edgartown

Normans Land

Martha's
Vineyard

Nantuck

Nantuck

ATLANTIC
OCEAN

Symbol	Description	Symbol	Description	Symbol	Description
	Interstate		State Capital		State Forest
	Major Highway		Highest Point in State		National Park
	Appalachian Trail		Mountains		National Wildlife Refuge
	City or Town		Historic Site		State Park
					Other Points of Interest

N
W E
S

miles
50

MASSACHUSETTS
★ MAP SKILLS ★

1. **What state forest is located on Martha's Vineyard?**

2. **Which interstate runs west-south through the state?**

3. **What is Massachusetts's southernmost island?**

4. **What point of interest is located south of Worcester?**

5. **Which river is located in the Berkshires?**

6. **What national wildlife refuge can you find in Northeast Massachusetts?**

7. **What is the name of the large reservoir that is located in the middle of the state?**

8. **What city is located on the tip of Cape Cod?**

9. **What two routes would you take to get from Pittsfield to Springfield?**

10. **What state park is located south of Quincy?**

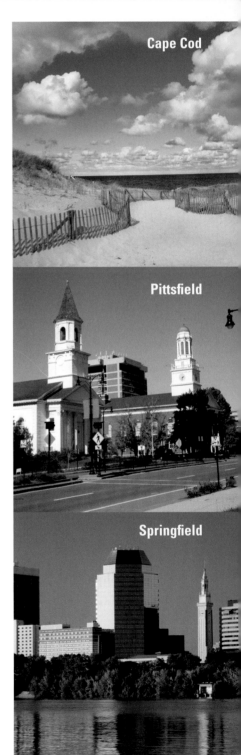

Cape Cod

Pittsfield

Springfield

10. Blue Hills Reservation
9. Routes 7 and 20
8. Provincetown
7. Quabbin Reservoir
6. Parker River National Wildlife Refuge
5. Housatonic River
4. Clara Barton Birthplace
3. Normans Land
2. Interstate 90
1. Manuel F. Correllus State Forest

State Seal, Flag, and Song

The Massachusetts state seal features the commonwealth's coat of arms. The star (silver instead of white) indicates that Massachusetts was one of the 13 original colonies. The state seal was made official on June 4, 1885. Beginning in 1894 there was an attempt to create a more accurate representation of the Native American on the seal. The Native American was redesigned, and in 1898, Edmund H. Garrett's design was made the official representation of the coat of arms for Massachusetts.

The state flag of Massachusetts features the coat of arms of the commonwealth—showing a Native American holding a bow and arrow, with the arrow pointing downward to indicate that the Native American is peaceful. The background and a star in the coat of arms are white. The state motto is written in Latin on a ribbon beneath the coat of arms. The motto translates to "By the Sword We Seek Peace, but Peace Only Under Liberty."

To see the lyrics of the Massachusetts State Song, "All Hail to Massachusetts,"
go to **www.statesymbolsusa.org/Massachusetts/Song_mass.html**

Glossary

ammunition The objects (such as bullets and shells) that are shot from weapons.

ancestors Relatives from the past.

committee A group of people who are chosen to do a particular job or to make decisions about something.

confederation A group of people, countries, organizations, etc., that are joined together in some activity or effort.

council A group of people who are chosen to make rules, laws, or decisions about something.

democracy A form of government in which people choose leaders by voting.

endangered In danger of no longer existing.

environmentalists People concerned about the quality of the environment, especially pollution.

famine A situation in which many people do not have enough food to eat.

immigrants People who come to a country to live there.

pharmaceuticals Drugs or medicine.

plantations Large areas of land, especially in hot parts of the world, where crops (such as cotton) are grown.

segregated Set apart or separated from others of the same kind or group.

seizures Abnormal states in which a person becomes unconscious and his/her body moves in uncontrolled and violent ways.

summit The highest level.

surveyed Measured and examined.

wharves Flat structures that are built along the shores of rivers, oceans, etc., so that ships can load and unload cargo or passengers.

More About Massachusetts

BOOKS

Cunningham, Kevin. *The Massachusetts Colony*. New York, NY: Scholastic, 2011.

Jackson, Shirley. *The Witchcraft of Salem Village*. New York, NY: Random House, 2011.

Keller, Susanna. *The True Story of Paul Revere's Ride*. New York, NY: PowerKids Press, 2013.

Malaspina, Ann. *The Boston Tea Party*. Minneapolis, MN: Abdo Publishing, 2013.

Truet, Trudi Strain. *Massachusetts (America the Beautiful)*. New York, NY: Scholastic, 2014.

WEBSITES

The Freedom Trail:

www.thefreedomtrail.org

New England Aquarium:

www.neaq.org

The Official Massachusetts Government Page:

www.mass.gov

Old Sturbridge Village:

www.osv.org

Plimoth Plantation:

www.plimoth.org

ABOUT THE AUTHORS

Ruth Bjorklund has written a number of books for young readers on topics ranging from states to animals to health issues. She has lived in the Berkshires, in Boston, and on Cape Cod. She is a former youth services librarian and shares her home on Bainbridge Island, Washington, with her husband, two children, and their pets.

Stephanie Fitzgerald has been writing nonfiction for children for more than 10 years, and she is the author of more than 20 books. Her specialties include history, wildlife, and popular culture. She lives in Stamford, Connecticut, with her husband and their daughter.

Index

Page numbers in **boldface** are illustrations.

Index